Sunday in the South

"I know that nothing is better for them than to rejoice, and to do good in their lives, and also that every man should eat and drink and enjoy the good of all his labor - it is the gift of God."

– Solomon
  Ecclesiastes 3:12

Sunday in the South

© 2011, 2nd edition

© 2010 by Ginny McCormack

Website: www.ginnymccormackcooks.com

Email: contactginnymccormack@gmail.com

Photography by Noah Maier

www.noahmaierphotography.com

Published in the United States by His Kids Publishing, Inc.

www.hiskidspublishing.com

All scripture taken from *The Holy Bible*, New International Version ©1973, 1978, 1984 International Bible Society

Every effort has been made to provide proper and accurate source attribution for quotations used in this book. Should any attributions be found to be incorrect, the author and publisher welcome written documentation supporting correction for subsequent printings.

ISBN 978-0-9720417-6-8

Cover, interior and floral design by Ginny McCormack

Recipe development and food styling by Ginny McCormack

Printed in China

Sunday in the South

Ginny McCormack

Photography by Noah Maier

Cover, interior, floral design, recipe development
and food styling by Ginny McCormack

HIS KIDS
PUBLISHING, INC.

Sunday, a Day of Delight

"Being who is the Beneficent Author of all the good that was, that is, that will be; We unite in rendering unto Him our sincere and humble thanks for His kind care and protection and for the great degree of tranquility, union and plenty which we have enjoyed; We most humbly offer...our prayers and supplications to the Great Lord and Ruler of Nations."

– George Washington (1732-1789)
   First American president

"A world without a Sabbath would be like a man without a smile, like a summer without flowers, and like a homestead without a garden. It is the most joyous day of the whole week."

– Henry Ward Beecher (1813-1887)
   American clergyman

" 'Therefore I urge you to take nourishment, for this is for your survival, since not a hair will fall from the head of any of you.' And when he had said these things, he took bread and gave thanks to God in the presence of them all; and when he had broken it he began to eat. Then they were all encouraged, and also took food themselves."

– Paul
   Acts 27:33-36

"There is no better time or place to build friendships than around the joy-filled, warm and inviting table we set for friends on Sunday."

– Russell Cronkhite
   Chef and author

"Give us food, enough for well-being. Give us grace and strength to forebear and persevere. Give us courage and gaiety and the quiet mind. Spare to us our friends, soften to us our enemies."

– Robert Louis Stevenson (1850-1894)
   Scottish poet and essayist

Sunday morning, 1947, Auburndale, Florida

For Judy Wahlbom, the little girl in this picture, who grew up to be a Godly woman, a devoted wife, a wonderful mother and a great cook. Thank you for teaching me what your mother taught you – that cooking for others is the sincerest expression of love.

Your daughter,

Ginny

Introduction

It was not until I became an adult, with a family of my own, that I began to fully appreciate the significance of those Sunday dinners of my childhood. They were happy, noisy occasions. Upon returning home from church, we were greeted at the door by the savory aroma of a pot roast that had been slowly simmering in the oven all morning. My mother, still wearing her Sunday dress, would exchange her high-heeled shoes for comfortable slippers and hurry around the kitchen as she busily prepared the rice, tossed the salad and sweetened the iced tea. I would set the table with the special placemats, good china, and cloth napkins. We would join hands and bow our heads in prayer as my father thanked God for His provision, His protection and His unending love. Anticipation was high as we filled our plates with the familiar comfort foods we all adored. Although not specifically spoken, it was understood that the Sunday meal was different. It had a unique feel that differed from ordinary weekday meals. We felt a sense of respect for this treasured time we shared together. The sights, sounds and aromas were reliably comforting. We were together as a family. It was a safe and accepting place to be, a respite from the everyday busyness of life. It is unlikely I fully understood how meaningful these experiences were and how they would influence my life. At that time I only knew that the food was delicious, the conversation was lively, and I was a part of something special.

I am, as so many others are, a busy person with many responsibilities, not the least of which is caring for a large family. With weekends full of a variety of activities and commitments, it is so easy for Sunday dinner to get pushed aside or relegated to a drive-thru. I have come to accept that not every Sunday dinner will receive the attention to detail it likely deserves. My family often gathers with friends after church at a local restaurant or enjoys Sunday dinner in a variety of nontraditional ways. It might be take-out deli sandwiches on the back porch or a simple picnic at a soccer game. Although our busy, modern lives may prevent us from regularly gathering for a traditional Sunday dinner, we would be depriving ourselves greatly if we abandoned it altogether. Great joy can come from the connection we feel with such time-honored traditions. I encourage you to gather your family and create new memories around your Sunday dinner table. In my home, it is an all-hands-on affair. I have found that children appreciate the end result far more if they have been involved in the process. Everyone can play a part, whether it be arranging the flowers, setting the table, or stirring the gravy. Then, as loved ones come together at the table to dine and fellowship, they will inevitably sense they are a part of something greater than just a meal. They are a part of Sunday Dinner.

Ginny McCormack

Table of Contents

A Mid Summer Luncheon

The Menu

Citrus Marinated Chicken

Creamy Corn Pudding

Spinach and Walnut Salad with Orange Vinaigrette

Mile High Magic Cookie Bars

"Eating is not merely a material pleasure. Eating well gives a spectacular joy to life and contributes immensely to goodwill and happy companionship. It is of great importance to the morale."

– Elsa Schiaparelli (1890–1973)
Italian Designer

As the weather grows warmer, my favorite backyard hydrangea bush bursts into bloom with much anticipated glory. Those billowy blossoms are then transformed into one of my favorite - and simplest - centerpieces. Try tying back the curtains and opening the blinds so your Sunday dinner table is bathed in natural sunlight. Pure white serving pieces are a classic and versatile touch. They pair beautifully with clear glasses, vases and votive candle holders which reflect both the natural light and candlelight in the room. A touch of robin's egg blue on the dinner plates keeps the theme soft and summery.

"Glass is an honest medium; it conceals nothing, but reflects everything."

    - Carolyne Roehm
      Author and entertaining expert

A Breath of Fresh Hydrangeas

*W*hat makes hydrangeas so irresistible? Those enormous, cloud-like blossoms are familiar warm weather friends. Grouped in a garden basket or displayed in clear glass vases, these angelic flowers are a heavenly presence on your dinner table. If you don't have one, consider adding a hydrangea bush to your garden. It will grant you a multitude of gorgeous blooms for many years to come.

Display your beautiful hydrangea blossoms individually in clear glass vases filled with glass stones. The stones provide support for the stems and also reflect light, creating a beautiful effect. (1) Carefully fill each vase with decorative glass stones, available at craft stores. (2) Measure the height of the blossom to the vase and trim the stem diagonally. (3) Fill the vase with water, and (4) add a few drops of chlorine bleach to keep the water clear and clean.

Simple Citrus Marinade

Bursting with flavor, this super simple marinade is a snap to make. Combine equal amounts of soy sauce, lemon juice and orange marmalade. I typically use 1 or ½ cup of each, depending on the amount of meat I am marinating. Pour over chicken, beef or pork and refrigerate in an airtight container or sealed plastic bag for 2-6 hours. The longer you marinate, the more intense the flavor will be.

Citrus Marinated Chicken

Whether grilled or roasted, this citrus-infused chicken is full of flavor. It is even delicious served cold the next day or shredded and placed atop a salad. I occasionally substitute lime juice for lemon juice in the marinade, resulting in a stronger citrus flavor.

12-14 boneless chicken thighs, skin on
1 cup soy sauce
1 cup orange marmalade
1 cup lemon juice
salt and pepper

Place the chicken in a zip loc bag or container with a lid. Combine the soy sauce, orange marmalade and lemon juice. Pour the marinade over the chicken. Seal the container and refrigerate for 2 hours or longer.

For grilling:
Rub the grill with oil to avoid sticking. Preheat the grill to medium high heat. Remove the chicken from the marinade, sprinkle with salt and pepper and grill, skin side down, for 6-8 minutes. Flip the chicken and cook an additional 4-6 minutes or until the juices run clear.

For roasting:
Preheat oven to 400 degrees. Remove the chicken from the marinade, sprinkle with salt and pepper and place in a shallow baking pan, skin side up. Roast for 25-30 minutes or until the juices run clear.

Discard any unused marinade.

Makes 6-8 servings

Creamy Corn Pudding

Golden and bubbly as it emerges from the oven, this cheesy side dish has all the characteristics of comfort food. It calls for frozen white creamed corn, which is a fresh tasting alternative to canned corn. It is sold in rolls in your grocer's freezer section.

2 rolls frozen white creamed corn, thawed

½ stick butter, melted

3 Tbsp. sugar

½ cup milk

1 cup cheddar cheese, grated

2 Tbsp. flour

3 eggs, beaten

Preheat oven to 350 degrees.

In a medium bowl, combine all ingredients. Pour into a greased 2 quart baking dish. Bake for 45 minutes or until set and golden.

Makes 8 servings

"South of the Border" Variation:
- Add 1 small can chopped green chiles
- Substitute Mexican blend cheese for the cheddar cheese

How I love a great vinaigrette. The melding of two distinctly unique partners, oil and vinegar, lends proof to the adage that opposites attract. The addition of herbs, sugar, salt, spices or citrus juice can transform this simple dressing into a culinary masterpiece - perfect for drizzling on fresh greens or marinating fish and poultry.

The Art of the Vinaigrette

Oil is the soul of your dressing. Most vegetable oils make a fine vinaigrette. Canola, safflower and soybean oil are light in flavor, while olive oil is deeper and more complex. Walnut, sesame and avocado oil are darker and more intense.

If oil is the soul, then vinegar is the heart of your vinaigrette. White wine vinegar is reliably mild and versatile. Sherry, raspberry and cider vinegars produce full-flavored vinaigrettes. The dark, sweet flavor of balsamic vinegar is sublime.

Citrus juice makes a fabulous addition to your vinaigrette. Due to its high acid content, it can easily replace part of the vinegar in your recipe. Lemon and lime juice will kick up the flavor, while orange juice will provide more sweetness.

Be sure to give your vinaigrette a sprinkling of salt and pepper. Even if you add no additional seasonings to your dressing, salt and pepper are essential, as they will enhance the flavor of your ingredients.

The choices of herbs and seasonings for your vinaigrette are endless. Fresh chopped basil, oregano, thyme, and parsley are great choices. Each herb will lend its unique flavor and pleasantly alter the character of your dressing.

Dried herbs pair well with vinaigrettes. They are highly concentrated compared to fresh herbs, so you will only need to use one-third as much. Garlic, mustard and sugar are also nice additions to your vinaigrette.

What is the perfect oil to vinegar ratio for a fabulous vinaigrette? Traditionally, a 3:1 ratio will produce a classic, smooth vinaigrette. A 2:1 ratio will yield a vinaigrette that is slightly thinner and more tart. Experiment with the proportions until you find your favorite.

Oil and vinegar do not really want to combine with one another. It is a classic love-hate relationship. *Temporary emulsion* is the term used to describe what occurs when you vigorously shake to combine oil and vinegar. An airtight jar with a tight lid is best for this job.

Homemade vinaigrette may be stored in the refrigerator for 3-4 weeks. Use it to dress your fresh greens, vegetable salads, or to marinate meat, fish or poultry. Try sampling new oils, vinegars, and the limitless array of herbs and seasonings to create your own signature vinaigrette.

Spinach and Walnut Salad with Orange Vinaigrette

I sometimes make seasonal substitutions or additions to this delicious salad recipe by including chopped apples, sliced strawberries or dried cranberries.

6–8 cups fresh spinach or 1 (9 oz.) bag fresh spinach, torn into pieces
½ cup walnuts, coarsely chopped
1 can mandarin orange segments, drained
½ medium red onion, sliced thinly
1 Tbsp. butter, melted

Dressing:
½ cup canola or vegetable oil
¼ cup orange juice
4 Tbsp. white wine vinegar
3 Tbsp. sugar
1 tsp. salt

Preheat oven to 350 degrees.
Toss the walnuts with the melted butter and spread on a baking sheet. Toast in the oven for 8–10 minutes or until golden brown. Watch carefully to avoid burning. Allow to cool before using.

Place the spinach, walnuts, mandarin oranges and red onion in a large salad bowl.

Combine the oil, orange juice, vinegar, sugar and salt in a jar with a tight fitting lid. Shake vigorously to combine.

Toss the salad with enough of the dressing to coat. Store leftover dressing in the refrigerator.

Makes 6 servings

Mile High Magic Cookie Bars

This is a ramped up version of the much beloved magic cookie bar recipe. Many of the filling ingredients are doubled, creating a magic cookie bar that is twice as high and twice as yummy. White chocolate, butterscotch, or peanut butter chips may be substituted for part or all of the chocolate chips.

1 ½ cups graham cracker crumbs

½ cup butter, melted

3 Tbsp. sugar

2 (3 ½ oz.) cans shredded coconut

2 cans sweetened condensed milk

2 cups pecans, chopped

2 cups semisweet chocolate chips

Preheat oven to 350 degrees.

In a small bowl, combine the graham cracker crumbs, butter and sugar. Press firmly into the bottom of a 9 x 13-inch baking pan. Spread the chopped pecans over the crumbs, followed by the chocolate chips and shredded coconut. Pour the condensed milk evenly over the top.

Bake 30-35 minutes or until the edges are golden brown. Cool before slicing.

Makes 18 servings

A Formal Sunday Feast

The Menu

Standing Rib Roast with Horseradish Cream

Roasted Fingerling Potatoes

Iceberg Wedge with Chunky Blue Cheese Dressing

Dark Chocolate Cream Pie

"Food is our common ground, a universal experience."

– James Beard (1903 – 1985)
American chef and food writer

An Elegant Table

*T*here is no need to wait for a special occasion to enjoy your beautiful wedding china and crystal glassware. Why not dust off your grandmother's candlesticks and give them a place of honor on your Sunday dinner table? Any Sunday can be a good day to create a memorable meal by enlisting the help of those often neglected, yet treasured, items such as fine china, crystal, silver and linens. The new mood you create at Sunday dinner will not soon be forgotten. If you wish to begin or add to your china collection, yard sales and estate sales provide wonderful opportunities to pick up beautiful pieces at bargain prices.

*F*uchsia spray roses (below) spill from a silver serving bowl to adorn the Sunday dinner table. By laying my grandmother's cut linen tablecloth on the table several days in advance, many of the wrinkles fell out and I avoided having to iron or steam it. Liquid silver cleaner quickly brought back the radiance to these old silver pieces. The liquid version, which sponges on and rinses off, is quicker to use than the cream variety.

*T*he antique buffet in the dining room (opposite, top) accommodates a beautiful dinner presentation. Utilizing the buffet allows for easy self service and prevents the dining table from becoming crowded with serving dishes.

"The only thing that separates us from the animals is our ability to accessorize."

– Clairee Belcher
Steel Magnolias, 1989

A standing rib roast, also known as prime rib, is one of the eight primal cuts of beef. It is comprised of up to seven ribs and is referred to as "standing" because it is most often roasted in a standing position. Its reputation as a superior cut of beef is well deserved.

Preparing the Roast

To ensure that slicing and serving the roast is an easy proposition, I like to separate the meat from the bones prior to roasting. Your grocer's butcher will be happy to do this for you, or you can make quick work of it with a sharp chef's knife (Fig. 1). Though separated from the roast, the bones should remain in place during roasting as they contribute immensely to the flavor and tenderness of the roast. Use butcher's or kitchen twine to securely tie the bones and roast together (Fig. 2).

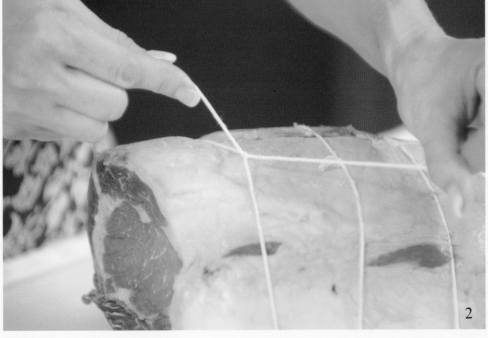

Standing Rib Roast with Horseradish Cream

"20 minutes to the pound, plus 20 minutes more," is a phrase I heard my grandmother repeat time and again when referring to how to roast prime rib to the perfect medium rare. If you prefer a more scientific method, use a meat thermometer to ensure your roast is 130-135 degrees for rare, 140-145 for medium rare and 150-160 for medium. Due to its tenderness, prime rib is typically "dry heat" roasted, meaning it is not covered and liquid is not added to the roasting pan.

1 standing rib roast of beef, approximately 5-7 lbs.
salt and pepper

Preheat oven to 350 degrees.
Line a roasting pan with aluminum foil. Prepare the roast if it has not already been separated from the bone *(see page 37)*. Generously salt and pepper the roast and place it in the roasting pan. Bake 20 minutes per pound, plus 20 minutes more for a medium rare roast, or 2 hours, 20 minutes for a 6 lb. roast. Allow the roast to rest for 20 minutes before carving. Serve with Horseradish Cream.

Makes 8-10 servings

Horseradish Cream
In a small bowl, combine:
½ cup sour cream
3 Tbsp. prepared horseradish
½ tsp. Salt
dash of pepper

"Vegetables are interesting but lack a sense of purpose when unaccompanied by a good cut of meat."

- Fran Lebowitz
  American author

Roasted Fingerling Potatoes

Fingerling potatoes belong to a family referred to as "heritage" or "heirloom" potatoes. This means they have been openly pollinated and in existence for more than 50 years. Heirloom potatoes come in a variety of colors such as red, yellow and purple. I typically purchase a 2 lb. bag of mixed fingerling potatoes for this recipe which gives me a nice assortment of color. They have a rich, nutty flavor and, when roasted, the edges of the potatoes will crisp up while the interior remains smooth and creamy.

1 (2 lb.) bag mixed fingerling potatoes, or 2 lbs. baby Yukon gold or red potatoes, cut into medium size chunks
1 medium onion, chopped
4 Tbsp. olive oil
kosher salt
pepper

Preheat oven to 450 degrees.
Place potatoes and onion on a large baking sheet or pan. Drizzle with olive oil and toss until thoroughly coated. Sprinkle generously with salt and pepper. Roast 25–30 minutes or until tender, tossing once during roasting.

Makes 6 servings

Iceberg Wedge with Chunky Blue Cheese Dressing

This crisp "fork and knife" salad is a classic pairing for a standing rib roast.

2 heads fresh iceberg lettuce, quartered

1 (4 oz.) container crumbled blue or gorgonzola cheese

4 slices bacon, cooked until crisp and chopped coarsely

1 medium tomato, seeded and chopped

Place iceberg wedges on 8 individual salad plates. Drizzle *Chunky Blue Cheese Dressing* over each wedge and sprinkle each with blue cheese, crumbled bacon, and chopped tomato.

Chunky Blue Cheese Dressing

In a blender, process until smooth:

½ cup mayonnaise

½ cup sour cream

1/3 cup milk

1 (4 oz.) container crumbled blue or gorgonzola cheese

½ tsp. salt

2 tsp. lemon juice

Makes 8 servings

Dark Chocolate Cream Pie

This old fashioned cream pie is lusciously rich and full of of deep chocolate flavor. I typically make two, as one seems never enough for a family of chocolate lovers. Try the Classic Pie Crust recipe (p. 55) or opt for a prepared, refrigerated crust.

1 (9") pie crust, pre baked

1 ¼ cups sugar

¼ cup cornstarch

½ tsp. salt

3 cups whole milk

4 egg yolks, beaten

3 oz. unsweetened chocolate, chopped

¼ cup (½ stick) butter

1 tsp. pure vanilla extract

1 pint whipping cream

¼ cup sugar

1 oz. semisweet chocolate, shaved

> ### How to Pre Bake a Pie Crust
>
> *Preheat the oven to 350 degrees. Line the pie crust with parchment paper, aluminum foil or a large coffee filter. Fill the crust half full with pie weights, rice or beans. Bake 20 minutes, remove the weights, prick the bottom of the crust several times with a fork and bake for an additional 5-10 minutes. Cool completely before filling.*

Combine sugar, cornstarch and salt in a large saucepan. Add the milk and chocolate and cook over medium high heat until the chocolate is melted and the mixture is slightly thickened. Reduce heat and continue cooking for 4 minutes. Remove from heat.

To the beaten eggs, add about ½ cup of the chocolate mixture and stir. Add the eggs to the saucepan, bring to a low boil and stir continuously for 4 minutes. Stir in the butter and vanilla. Pour into the baked pie crust, cool, and chill for 2-3 hours. Place the whipping cream in the bowl of an electric stand mixer. Add the sugar and whip the cream until soft peaks form. Spread the cream over the top of the chilled pie and garnish with the chocolate shavings.

Makes 8 servings

"All I really need is love, but a little chocolate now and then doesn't hurt!"

– Lucy Van Pelt
Peanuts by Charles M. Schulz

"The sights, sounds and smells of beauty are all around us. When we take the time to observe even the simplest things, we should be mindful of their power to inspire us."

- G.M.

A Casual Evening Supper

The Menu

Savory Sausage and Mushroom Quiche

Red Raspberry Gelatin Salad

Sweet English Peas with Caramelized Shallots

Fresh Apple Cake with Hot Buttered Rum Sauce

"The chief pleasure in eating does not consist in costly seasoning, or exquisite flavor, but in yourself."

– Horace (65–8 B.C.)
  Roman lyric poet

The Feel of Home

$\mathcal{F}$ew things are as appealing as a simple family dinner, served from the hearthside coffee table with plates in laps - no dining table required. Perhaps it's the obvious lack of fussiness, or the predominance of comfort food associated with this kind of gathering that is so enjoyable. A simple menu, a comfortable place to relax, and some lively conversation are all that is required for this memorable Sunday dinner.

"A man seldom thinks with more earnestness of anything than he does of his dinner."

– Samuel Johnson (1709–1784)
  English author

$\mathcal{D}$innertime is delightful when it's an all-hands-on family affair. Even the littlest pair of hands can shell the peas, measure the flour for the cake, or set the table. When mine were little they loved to be in charge of collecting fresh flowers from the yard to place in tiny vases for the dinner table.

$\mathcal{S}$easonal fruits and vegetables make simple yet lovely presentations on your counters and table. The Pink Lady apples (below) will likely last an hour or two before someone snatches them up for an afternoon snack.

A simple arrangement of lilacs, hypericum berries and lemon leaves compliment the table with hues of green and white.

A rich, warm quiche is a comforting proposition. The idea of filling a flaky pie crust with a harmonious blend of eggs, cream and cheese is simply inspired. I was raised on this dependable quiche recipe, although it was a slightly altered version. It was simply referred to as Ham Quiche, which is similar to Quiche Lorraine. What makes quiche such a culinary all-star is its versatility. It can be filled with any number of delectable ingredients: bacon, ham, seafood, spinach, broccoli, and a variety of cheeses. The possibilities are endless. This Savory Sausage and Mushroom Quiche is a delicious incarnation.

Classic Pie Crust

Purchase a ready-made pie crust or make a homemade one? That is the question - and a common dilemma faced by many cooks as they contemplate a basketful of apples just begging to be transformed into an apple pie. If time is on your side, then roll up your sleeves and use this simple recipe to create a deliciously flaky crust worthy of your best quiche, fruit pie or pot pie recipe.

Recipe for 2 crusts:

2 ½ cups all purpose flour, plus more for sprinkling

1 cup (2 sticks) butter

½ tsp. salt

4-8 Tbsp. ice water

1. Cut the butter into small cubes and place in the freezer for 10 minutes until thoroughly chilled.

2. Using a food processor or a bowl and pastry cutter, combine the flour and salt. Add the butter and pulse, or cut, until the mixture resembles coarse meal with pea size pieces of butter. Adding 1 Tbsp. of water at a time, work the mixture until it begins to clump together. Pinch a piece between your fingers and if it holds together, it is ready. Do not overwork. The pieces of butter you see in the dough are essential to a flaky crust.

3. Remove the dough and divide it into 2 parts, shaping each portion into a flat disk. Dust with a little flour, wrap with plastic wrap and chill each disk in the refrigerator for one hour (may be kept chilled up to 3 days).

4. Remove one disk from the refrigerator and let rest 5-10 minutes. Place on a well floured work surface and sprinkle with additional flour. Using a rolling pin, roll the dough into a 12-inch circle about 1/8-inch thick. Use more flour as needed to avoid sticking.

5. Carefully lift the dough and place it in a 9-inch pie plate. Press it gently so it lines the bottom and sides of the plate. Use a sharp knife or kitchen shears the edge of the dough, leaving a ½-inch overhang. For a single pie crust, fold the edges under and flute them using your thumb and forefinger or use a fork to create a decorative edge. (For a double pie crust, repeat step 4 with the second disk. After filling the pie, gently lay the second crust on top. Fold the top crust over and under the edge of the bottom crust. Press the edges together and flute them. Cut four slits in the center of the top crust to allow the steam to escape. Bake as instructed.

A Simple Shortcut

Ready-made pie crusts have come a very long way. A few brands are even flaky and buttery enough to rival their homemade counterparts. This is great news for home cooks, who have a perfectly acceptable - and delicious - alternative to a from-scratch crust.

Homemade Mayonnaise

I suspect very few of us have entertained the idea of preparing homemade mayonnaise. With the availability of so many acceptable commercial varieties, I also subscribed to the "why would I bother?" line of thinking. That all changed after I indulged in my first taste of this creamy homemade mixture of eggs, oil, lemon juice and salt. Mayonnaise is an uncomplicated condiment, yet it is a culinary workhorse, enhancing dishes like quiche, casseroles, dressings, dips, sandwiches and tuna, chicken, and egg salads. The fresh, rich flavor of this homemade mayonnaise is worth the few minutes it will take to whip up a batch. You might even try kicking up the flavor with the addition of fresh, chopped herbs, garlic, chili powder, cayenne pepper or mustard.

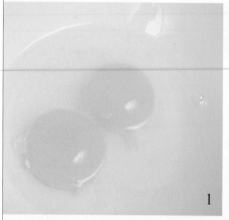

2 large eggs

2 cups canola or vegetable oil

2 Tbsp. lemon juice

1 tsp. salt

Place eggs in a medium size mixing bowl (Fig. 1). Add lemon juice (Fig. 2). Using a hand held mixer on medium speed with one hand, begin to slowly drizzle the oil into the eggs with the other hand (Fig. 3). For the mixture to properly emulsify, be sure to drizzle the oil slowly. Pause to add the salt (Fig. 4). Increase mixer speed to medium high and continue mixing as the mayonnaise emulsifies and thickens (Fig. 5). The end result will be a smooth and creamy mayonnaise (Fig. 6) suitable for dipping, spreading or adding to recipes like the *Savory Sausage and Mushroom Quiche.*

Savory Sausage and Mushroom Quiche

Reliably delicious, this versatile quiche recipe never disappoints. Served any time of day, it is both a breakfast and dinner favorite in my home. Use the Classic Pie Crust recipe on p. 55 or opt for a prepared, refrigerated pie crust.

1 (9-inch) unbaked pie crust

8 oz. bulk pork sausage, browned and drained

1 small carton baby portobello mushrooms, chopped

¾ cup Swiss cheese, grated

¾ cup cheddar cheese, grated

½ cup milk

2 eggs

½ cup mayonnaise

1 Tbsp. cornstarch

Preheat oven to 350 degrees. Prepare pie crust in a 9-inch pie pan.

In a large bowl, whisk together milk, eggs, mayonnaise and cornstarch until smooth. Add sausage, mushrooms and cheeses and combine thoroughly. Pour mixture into pie crust and bake 45 minutes or until golden.

Makes 6-8 servings

Red Raspberry Gelatin Salad

This cool and fruity dish may change your opinion of gelatin salads. It's fruity sweetness pairs beautifully with the Savory Sausage and Mushroom Quiche. With just three ingredients, it is quick and simple to prepare. Try presenting it in a clear glass serving dish and garnishing it with fresh red raspberries and mint leaves. Simple never looked so good.

1 large (6 oz.) package raspberry gelatin
1 (16 oz.) bag frozen raspberries
2 cups applesauce

In a serving dish, dissolve gelatin in 2 cups hot water. Add raspberries and applesauce and stir gently to combine. Chill 3–4 hours or until set.

Makes 8 servings

"*Slightly tart and sassy, raspberries are a fruit with real attitude, but one you can't help loving immensely.*"
-G.M.

Sweet English Peas with Caramelized Shallots

Full of sweet flavor and earthy goodness, freshly shelled English peas are a culinary delight. They enjoy a relatively short growing season, so keep an eye out for them in late spring and early summer.

3 lbs. English peas in the pods, shelled and rinsed (about 3 cups) or 3 cups frozen peas
1 tsp. salt
3 large shallots, finely chopped
3 Tbsp. butter

Place peas in a medium saucepan with just enough water to cover them. Add the salt and bring to a boil over medium high heat. Boil 5–6 minutes or until tender. Drain and set aside.

Melt the butter in a large skillet over medium high heat. Add the shallots and saute until tender and golden. Add the peas to the skillet, toss to coat and cook for 1–2 minutes until heated through.

Makes 4–6 servings

Fresh Apple Cake with Hot Buttered Rum Sauce

This chunky cake, brimming with chopped apples and walnuts, is always a crowd pleaser. Drizzled with sweet Hot Buttered Rum Sauce, it becomes simply irresistible. The sauce is also delicious served over vanilla ice cream.

½ cup (1 stick) butter, softened

2 cups sugar

2 eggs

2 cups all purpose flour

1 tsp. baking powder

1 tsp. baking soda

½ tsp. salt

½ tsp. nutmeg

½ tsp. cinnamon

½ cup walnuts, chopped

4 medium to large apples, peeled, cored and chopped.

Preheat oven to 350 degrees. Generously grease a tube pan.

In a large bowl, combine butter and sugar until light and fluffy. Add eggs and combine. In another bowl, whisk together flour, baking powder, baking soda, salt, nutmeg and cinnamon. Gradually add to egg mixture, combining thoroughly. Stir in apples and nuts. Mixture will be very thick. Scrape batter into the tube pan and bake 45–50 minutes, or until a toothpick inserted in the center comes out clean. Cool 15 minutes and then invert cake onto a serving plate. Serve warm or room temperature. Spoon *Hot Buttered Rum Sauce* over individual slices when serving.

Makes 12 servings

Hot Buttered Rum Sauce

Combine in a small saucepan over medium heat until smooth and hot:

1 cup sugar

½ cup (1 stick) butter

½ cup light cream or half-n-half

1 tsp. rum extract

A 'Comfort Food' Family Dinner

The Menu

Carolina Crispy Fried Chicken Cutlets

Sour Cream Whipped Potatoes with Chive Butter

Chilled Marinated Asparagus Spears

Hot Buttered Croissants

Gooey Chocolate Fudge Cake

"If more of us valued food and cheer and song above hoarded gold, it would be a merrier world."

– J.R.R. Tolkien (1892-1973)

English author and poet

𝒜 visually appealing Sunday dinner table needn't be fussy or complicated. Classic blue and white dinnerware and flower pots can be paired with clear glassware and white linen napkins to create a dinner table that is simple, inviting and uncluttered.

Dressed in Blue

Blue and white porcelain, or "wares", originated in 9th century China. By the early 17th century much of it was imported to Europe and America where it was highly prized for its beauty and function. As European production of blue and white porcelain and pottery increased, it continued to be influenced by Chinese design, as well as reflect images of European culture. Today, a table setting of classic blue and white china remains a timeless image of beauty.

A Welcome Guest

*W*hat is your favorite comfort food? Each of us will likely answer that question differently. For me, a perfect example would be the Gooey Chocolate Fudge Cake in this chapter. For you, it might be a warm bowl of cheese grits, a slice of banana cream pie, or a heaping serving of your grandmother's squash casserole. Regardless of our choices, all comfort foods have several things in common. In general, comfort food is simply prepared and gives a sense of well-being. It is typically associated with our younger, formative years and evokes feelings and memories of home. The recipes are often treasured family heirlooms, passed down from one generation to the next. It is no wonder that comfort food is such a welcome guest at nearly every Sunday dinner table.

From the Nursery to the Table to the Garden

Rarely do my garden store purchases go directly into my garden. As with these purple Angelonia and white New Guinea impatiens, they often make an appearance on my dinner table first. Rather than purchasing a cut flower arrangement, transfer your plant purchases to decorative containers to adorn your table before planting them in the garden. Your flowers will be twice enjoyed.

Select your seasonal flowering plants and pair them with containers that will accommodate their size (Fig. 1). Vases, bowls, baskets, and even teapots and mason jars can make a lovely statement. Here, the square blue and white vases and large bowl will compliment our table setting. Try using a larger plant or grouping several smaller ones together in a single container. If the plant is too tall, use a cutting board and serrated knife to trim the roots for a better fit (Fig. 2) before placing it in the container (Fig. 3).

Spanish Moss is not actually a moss, but a flowering plant that grows hanging from tree branches throughout much of the southeastern United States (Fig. 4). It is a useful and attractive addition to potted plants because it covers the soil and helps the plant retain moisture. Spread a thick layer of Spanish moss just below the last layer of leaves (Fig. 5 & 6). Spanish moss is reasonably priced and can be purchased in a variety of dyed colors.

"I perhaps owe having become a painter to flowers."

– Claude Monet (1840-1926)
French impressionist painter

A Simple Shortcut

A brushing of melted butter and a beautiful presentation will transform your favorite bakery croissants from ordinary - to heavenly. A pastry brush makes quick work of slathering butter. Place the croissants in a simple basket lined with a colorful cloth and the transformation is complete.

"All sorrows are less with bread."

- Miguel de Cervantes (1547-1616)
  Spanish novelist, poet and playwright

"A cook she certainly was, in the very bone and center of her soul. Not a chicken or turkey or duck in the barnyard but looked grave when they saw her approaching, and seemed evidently to be reflecting on their latter end; and certain it was that she was always meditating on trussing, stuffing and roasting, to a degree that was calculated to inspire terror in any reflecting fowl living."

(Description of Aunt Chloe in *Uncle Tom's Cabin*, 1852)

- Harriet Beecher Stowe (1811–1896)
  American abolitionist and author

No Fail Triple-Dip Method

This will likely be the only dipping method for frying you will ever need. It dependably produces a flavorful, crisp crust. I use three disposable aluminum pans, which I reuse many times. They are easy to clean and stack nicely for convenient storage.

This method works equally well for poultry or fish. A coating of flour in the first step will allow the egg wash to stick. Panko bread crumbs are located alongside regular bread crumbs in the grocery store. They are lighter and more flaky than traditional crumbs and produce a crust that is crisp and airy. For triple dipping 6-8 servings, place the following in three disposable aluminum pans:

Pan 1:   2 cups flour

Pan 2:   Whisk together 3 eggs and 1/3 cup water or milk

Pan 3:   3 cups Panko bread crumbs

Generously salt and pepper the chicken. Using a pair of tongs, dip each piece into the flour first (Fig. 1), followed by the egg wash (Fig. 2), and finally the bread crumbs (Fig. 3). I like to press the chicken firmly into the bread crumbs to ensure a thick coating.

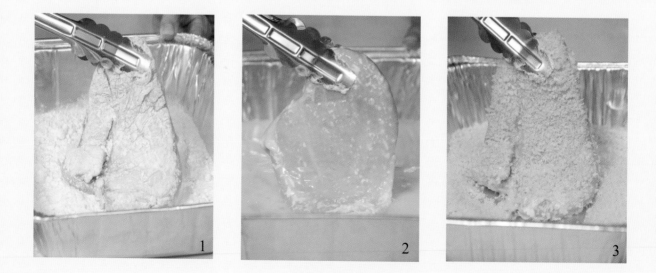

Carolina Crispy Fried Chicken Cutlets

Quintessentially southern, many regard fried chicken as the ultimate comfort food. I particularly enjoy the cutlets because of their versatility and quick cooking time. I sometimes serve them on large sandwich rolls or slice them and place them atop salads.

6 boneless, skinless chicken breasts
salt and pepper

Place the chicken between pieces of plastic wrap and pound to a thickness of 1/3 inch. Sprinkle generously with salt and pepper.

Fill a 10 to 12-inch heavy skillet with vegetable oil to a depth of ½ inch. Heat over medium high heat until hot but not smoking.

Prepare the chicken using the Triple Dip Frying Method *(opposite page)*. Fry the chicken two or three pieces at a time depending on size. To ensure proper browning, do not overcrowd the pan or allow the pieces to touch. Cook for 3–4 minutes per side.

Remove the chicken with metal tongs to a platter or cooling rack set over a baking sheet and place in a warm oven. Repeat this process with the remaining chicken.

Makes 6 servings

Chive Butter

Flavored butters are a delight. Adding dried or fresh chopped herbs, garlic, honey, citrus zest, or any other flavorful accompaniment will transform your butter from an everyday staple into a culinary treat. Try slathering your flavored butter onto mashed potatoes, baked potatoes, fresh steamed vegetables, warm biscuits or a slice of crusty french bread.

"Eat butter first, and eat it last, and live till a hundred years be past."

– Old Dutch proverb

1

2

This simple method begins with ½ cup (1 stick) fresh butter, slightly softened, and 2 Tbsp. chopped fresh chives (Fig. 1). Combine the two ingredients in a small mixing bowl (Fig. 2). Transfer the butter onto a piece of plastic wrap and fold the wrap over the top (Fig. 3). Gently roll the butter with your hands to form a log and twist the ends to seal (Fig. 4). Refrigerate until firm and serve.

3

4

Sour Cream Mashed Potatoes with Chive Butter

3 lbs. Yukon gold potatoes, peeled and quartered, or 3 lbs. refrigerated mashed potatoes

2 tsp. salt

¼ cup heavy cream

½ cup sour cream

¼ cup (½ stick) butter

salt and pepper

Place potatoes in a large pot with enough water to cover them. Add 2 tsp. salt and bring to a boil. Reduce heat, cover and simmer 20–30 minutes or until potatoes are fork tender. Drain the potatoes and return them to the pot. Warm the cream and butter in the microwave until the butter is melted and add them to the potatoes. Use a potato masher to mash the potatoes until they are smooth. Add the sour cream and stir the potatoes to the desired consistency, adding milk to thin if needed. Season to taste with salt and pepper. Do not over mix the potatoes or they will become sticky. Warm them over medium low heat until piping hot. Serve with Chive Butter.

Makes 8 servings

A Simple Shortcut

Believe it or not, there is a respectable alternative to mashing your own potatoes – and it does not involve a cardboard box. The emergence of fresh, refrigerated mashed potatoes on the market has given busy home cooks a reason to rejoice. I suggest purchasing the plain variety and adding your own butter, milk, sour cream and salt.

Chilled Marinated Asparagus Spears

Fresh or canned asparagus may be used for this delicious sweet and sour side dish. We enjoy this recipe year round and it graces nearly every holiday table. The asparagus is served cold and is marinated with a vinaigrette that is infused with cloves and cinnamon.

2 cans asparagus, drained

In a medium saucepan, combine the following and bring to a boil:

½ cup white vinegar

1 cup sugar

½ cup water

12 whole cloves

4 sticks cinnamon

1 tsp. salt

1 tsp. celery seed (optional)

Place asparagus in a flat container with a lid. As soon as the marinade comes to a boil, remove it from the heat and pour it over the asparagus. Cover and refrigerate 4-6 hours or overnight.

Makes 6 servings

"It is impossible to be ungrateful while eating chocolate cake."

- G.M.

Gooey Chocolate Fudge Cake

My mother was given this recipe by the mother of a girl in my 5th grade class. She brought a piece to school in her lunch box one day and I begged her relentlessly until she gave me a bite. It was definitely worth all that begging. We've been making it in my family for more than 35 years now.

2 cups sugar

2 cups all purpose flour

½ cup (1 stick) butter

3 ½ Tbsp. cocoa

1 cup water

½ cup oil

2 eggs

½ cup buttermilk

1 tsp. baking soda

1 tsp. pure vanilla extract

Preheat oven to 325 degrees.

In a large mixing bowl, combine the sugar and flour.

In a medium saucepan, heat the butter, cocoa, water and oil until butter is melted. Pour over the flour mixture and combine. Add the eggs, buttermilk, baking soda and vanilla. Mix well. Pour the batter into an ungreased 9 x 13-inch baking pan. Bake 35-40 minutes or until a toothpick inserted in the center comes out clean.

Icing

½ cup (1 stick) butter

1/3 cup milk

3 ½ Tbsp. cocoa powder

1 box confectioner's sugar

In a medium saucepan, heat butter, milk and cocoa over medium heat until butter is melted. Gradually add the confectioner's sugar and stir continuously until icing is smooth. Pour immediately over the hot cake.

Makes 12-16 servings

A Special Family Breakfast

The Menu

Georgia Pecan Pancakes with Sweet Peach Syrup

Brown Sugar Bacon

Cheesy Hash Brown Casserole

Fresh Berries with Vanilla Cream

Hot Coffee and Tangerine Spritzers

"All happiness depends on a leisurely breakfast."

- John Gunther (1901-1970)
American journalist

87

An "Any Time of Day" Meal

I suspect that my son's love for breakfast was initially born from the knowledge that this meal did not require him to consume a green vegetable of any kind. He later came to appreciate, as so many of us do, the undeniable appeal of waking to the smell of freshly brewed coffee and sizzling, hickory smoked bacon. Of course, any true breakfast lover knows that this delectable meal needn't be restricted to the morning hours. On the contrary, I've enjoyed some fabulous breakfasts, well, for dinner. *Georgia Pecan Pancakes* smothered in *Sweet Peach Syrup* are welcome in my home any time of day - or night.

I do myself a favor by setting the table the night before with my mother's casual Blue Danube china (opposite, top left). If we're feeling particularly civilized, I fill the creamer, sugar and coffee pot as we abandon the mugs for a day and opt for cups and saucers (opposite, top right). An open cabinet displays a small sampling of Blue Danube china (opposite, bottom left). This collection, acquired over many years, is a wonderful example of a truly versatile pattern, as lovely in a formal dinner setting as is for our cozy pancake breakfast. Handsome woven baskets and a whimsical pair of roosters adorn an antique bench in the corner of the breakfast room (opposite, lower right). Baskets are always a fine choice for kitchen decor, providing both beauty and function.

From the moment the first flowers were picked and placed on the first dinner table, man has sought a connection with the beauty of nature. Martin Luther recognized this beauty to be a divine expression when he wrote, "God writes the gospel not in the Bible alone, but on trees and flowers and clouds and stars." Is it any wonder we desire a closeness with such things of beauty?

What's in a Pot?

A straight row of clay garden pots lines the center of the breakfast table. Billowing with deep purple and lilac torinis, the presentation is fresh and lively. Clay pots are one of my favorite ways to decorate casual tables. They are affordable, come in an array of sizes, and can be easily transformed by sponging or spraying them with colored paint. Every Christmas I transfer my fresh poinsettias into large clay pots that I have sponged with gold metallic paint. Seasonal garden flowers are a natural pairing with clay pots. Pansies and torinis make a lovely late winter choice, while petunias, geraniums and begonias are spring and summer favorites.

" Look at us, said the violets blooming at her feet, all last winter we slept in seeming death but at the right time God awakened us, and here we are to comfort you."

- Edward Payson Roe (1838–1888)
American novelist

Sweet Peach Syrup

A perfect topping for pecan pancakes, this syrup is also delicious served over ice cream, cake, waffles, or even oatmeal.

1 ½ pounds fresh peaches, peeled & pitted,
 – *or* 1 (29 oz.) can sliced peaches in syrup
½ cup sugar
1 Tbsp. butter, melted

In a blender or food processor, puree peaches, sugar and butter until smooth.

Georgia Pecan Pancakes with Sweet Peach Syrup

These homemade pancakes combine the fluffy texture of traditional buttermilk pancakes with the hearty goodness of fresh pecans. Wait to sprinkle the pecans until after the pancakes are poured on the griddle so they remain on the surface and are toasted when the pancakes are flipped. Drizzle the pancakes generously with Sweet Peach Syrup for a flavor combination that is sublime. Double the recipe to serve 8.

2 cups all purpose flour

2 cups buttermilk

4 Tbsp. sugar

1 egg

1 ½ tsp. baking powder

1 tsp. baking soda

1 tsp. pure vanilla extract

¼ tsp. salt

1 ½ cups pecans, chopped

In a large mixing bowl, whisk together the flour, sugar, baking powder, baking soda and salt. Add the buttermilk, egg and vanilla. Whisk thoroughly to remove any lumps.

Preheat a griddle or large skillet over medium heat. Rub the griddle with oil to prevent sticking. Using a ladle, pour ½ cup portions of the batter onto the hot griddle. Sprinkle the pancakes with pecans and cook until bubbles appear on the surface and the pancake begins to set around the edges. Flip and cook until both sides are golden, about 3-4 minutes. Remove the pancakes to a platter in a warmed oven while you prepare the rest. Serve with Sweet Peach Syrup *(opposite page)*.

Makes 4 servings

Brown Sugar Bacon

A sprinkling of brown sugar is all it takes to transform ordinary bacon into something extra special. As it bakes, the sugar caramelizes and creates a sticky-sweet glaze that is nothing short of heavenly. It is so popular at my house that one pound is never enough.

1 lb. thick sliced, hickory smoked bacon
¼ cup brown sugar

Preheat oven to 375 degrees.
Line a large baking sheet with aluminum foil. Lay the strips of bacon on the baking sheet. They may overlap or touch a bit. Using your fingers, rub the brown sugar on top of the bacon. Place in the oven and bake 25–30 minutes or until the bacon is brown and slightly crisp. Serve immediately.

Makes 6-8 servings

"What I say is that, if a fellow really likes potatoes, he must be a pretty decent sort of fellow."

– A. A. Milne (1882–1956)
English author of the Winnie-the-Pooh series

Cheesy Hash Brown Casserole

Whether you prefer your hash browns cubed or shredded, this popular potato recipe is always a favorite. It has graced the table of nearly every southern potluck supper I have attended, and with good reason. Warm, cheesy and full of great potato flavor, it is comfort food at its best.

2 lbs. frozen hash brown potatoes, or 2 packages refrigerated hash brown potatoes

1 large onion, diced

1 (16 oz) carton sour cream

1 can cream of chicken soup

½ cup (1 stick) butter, melted

8 oz. sharp cheddar cheese, grated

1 tsp. salt

½ tsp. pepper

Topping:

4 cups corn flakes

½ cup (1 stick) butter, melted

Preheat oven to 350 degrees.

Spray a 9 x 13 baking pan with cooking spray. In a large mixing bowl, combine sour cream, cream of chicken soup and melted butter. Add hash brown potatoes, onion, cheddar cheese, salt and pepper. Mix thoroughly and spread in the baking pan. Place the corn flakes in a bowl and crush them. Add the melted butter and toss to coat. Spread the cornflakes evenly over the top of the casserole. Bake for 1 hour.

Makes 12 servings

South of the Border variation:

- *Purchase southwestern flavored refrigerated hash brown potatoes*
- *Substitute Mexican blend cheese for the cheddar cheese*
- *Add one small can green chiles*

Fresh Berries with Vanilla Cream

Fresh, seasonal berries are always a sweet treat and typically require no embellishment. In my home they are rinsed and usually eaten straight from the colander before they can be used for any other purpose. If there were only one way to improve upon the taste of fresh strawberries, raspberries and blackberries, it would likely be with a dollop of homemade sweet vanilla cream. It is a simple touch with a delicious impact.

1 lb. fresh strawberries, rinsed, stems removed and quartered

1 pint fresh raspberries, rinsed

1 pint fresh blackberries, rinsed

1 pint whipping cream, chilled

¼ cup sugar

1 tsp. pure vanilla extract

Combine berries and place in a serving bowl.

Place whipping cream, sugar and vanilla in a stand mixer with a whisk attachment and whip on medium high speed for 2–3 minutes or until soft peaks form. Serve *Sweet Vanilla Cream* alongside the fresh berries.

Makes 6–8 servings

Tangerine Spritzers

*This sparkling citrus punch is full of tangerine flavor and is a
refreshing alternative to orange juice.*

1 qt. tangerine juice
1 liter grapefruit or lemon–lime flavored carbonated soda
sliced oranges or maraschino cherries for garnish, optional

Chill the tangerine juice and soda. Combine them in a 2 quart
pitcher. Spritzers may be served alone or over ice. Garnish with
orange slices or cherries if desired.

Makes 8–10 servings

"The morning cup of coffee has an exhilaration about it which the cheering influence of the afternoon or evening cup of tea cannot be expected to reproduce."

- Oliver Wendell Holmes, Sr. (1841-1935)
  U.S. Supreme Court Justice

A Perfect Cup

*T*rue *coffee lovers know that the enjoyment associated with that perfect cup is a multi-sensory experience. The heavenly aroma of roasted coffee beans, the warmth of the cup in your hands, and the flavor of a perfect arabica blend are all reasons why coffee is the second most traded commodity in the world, second only to crude oil. The first credible account of coffee consumption was by 15th century monks in Yemen. Its popularity quickly spread throughout the globe where today it holds the title of most popular beverage in the world. Happily, there is an alternative to purchasing an overpriced 'coffee of the day' from the barista at your corner coffee shop. By following some simple guidelines, a perfect "cup o' joe" will be yours - for just pennies a serving. A few things to remember:*

1. <u>Choose only fresh, whole beans.</u> Arabica beans are the most popular in the U.S. By grinding only the beans you plan to use, you ensure your coffee will have the freshest, purest flavor possible. My coffee grinder cost less than $10 - and I say it's the best $10 I ever spent. Experiment with different bean varieties until you find your favorite. Store your beans in an airtight container in a dark, dry place. They will keep for a month.

2. <u>Use the best quality water available.</u> Since coffee is 98-99% water, you'll want to be sure your water is good tasting. Tap water is acceptable if it is free of the taste or smell of additives like chlorine or metals. A filtration device is an effective method for purifying tap water. Bottled water is also a nice alternative.

3. <u>Keep your additions pure.</u> At a mere 16 calories per teaspoon, pure cane sugar is my sweetener of choice. Unlike artificial sweeteners, its flavor has not been adulterated by chemicals and aftertastes. If you favor cream in your coffee, half-and-half and light cream are indulgences worth allowing. With only 40 calories and 3 grams of fat per 2 tablespoons, half-and-half is rich, creamy and full of pure dairy flavor. And by all means, never let a powdered dairy substitute near your coffee. Your superior "cup o' joe" will thank you.

A Seafood Lunch on the Porch

The Menu

Charleston Crispy Flounder with Apricot Chutney

Salt Crusted New Potatoes

Creamy Cole Slaw

White Cheddar Cornbread

Southern Key Lime Pie

"If you are ever at a loss to support a flagging conversation, introduce the subject of eating."

– Leigh Hunt (1784–1859)
  English critic and essayist

*W*hat a delight it is to dine al fresco on a beautiful Sunday afternoon. Inevitably, my family will linger longer at the table when dining outdoors. The fresh air and relaxed feel of dinner on the porch make for such a pleasant experience - and one we often repeat. Many are the times I've set my indoor table for dinner, only to hear someone make a declaration of how beautiful the weather is, followed by, "*Wouldn't it be nice to eat on the porch?*" On those occasions we typically grab our plates and head outside, a spontaneous reaction we never regret.

Many Ways with One Basket

Make a beautiful presentation on your Sunday dinner table by filling your favorite basket with an array of seasonal items. I prefer baskets that are low enough not to obstruct the view across the table. I apply stick-on felt pads to the bottom of the basket to protect the table from scratches. Rather than flowers, opt for other items such as fall leaves, mini pumpkins, gourds, apples, seasonal vegetables or fresh greenery. The basketful of citrus fruit for our 'Seafood Lunch on the Porch' holds extra limes from our Southern Key Lime Pie.

"An empty basket is an object with great potential. There it sits, waiting to be filled with any number of wonderful and interesting things."

G.M.

𝒜 good friend and native Mississippian once told me that no legitimate fish fry would ever be located more than one mile from "a good fishin' hole." That presents a bit of a challenge for someone like me. I'm relatively certain there is no such "hole" within close proximity of my suburban neighborhood, and if there was one, I'm not sure it would host the sort of water life I would want to serve my family for dinner. So I do what any good American home cook would do – and head to my grocery store's fish market. There I choose from a vast selection of beautiful seafood worthy of my *Crispy Flounder* recipe. By following a few simple steps, including the "triple dip" frying method, you can whip up a tasty, traditional fish fry – and never go near a "fishin' hole."

"In the hands of an able cook, fish can become an inexhaustible source of perpetual delight."

- Jeane Anthelme Brillat-Savarin (1755-1826)
French lawyer, politician and gastronome

Charleston Crispy Flounder with Apricot Chutney

A basket lined with brown parchment paper makes a nice presentation for fried fish. While flounder is the traditional choice for this low country favorite, I have also used halibut, cod, and even tilapia. Any mild tasting white fish will serve this recipe well. Do your little ones balk at the idea of eating fish? Do what I did and call it "water chicken." It worked, for today all of mine are fish lovers!

6 (6 oz.) flounder fillets
salt and pepper
vegetable oil for frying

Sprinkle the flounder fillets generously with salt and pepper. Fill a 10 to 12-inch skillet with oil to a depth of ½ inch. Heat the oil until hot, but not smoking. Prepare the flounder fillets using the *Triple Dip Method*. Place the following in three disposable aluminum pans:

Pan 1:   2 cups flour
Pan 2:   Whisk together 3 eggs and 1/3 cup water or milk
Pan 3:   3 cups panko bread crumbs

Generously salt and pepper the flounder. Using a pair of tongs, dip each fillet into the flour first, followed by the egg wash and then the bread crumbs. Press the fillets firmly into the bread crumbs to ensure a thick coating. Place the fillets, 2 or 3 at a time, into the hot oil and cook for 3 minutes on each side. To ensure proper browning, do not crowd the skillet. Using a separate pair of tongs, remove the fillets to a platter and place in a warm oven. Repeat this process with the remaining fillets. Serve with *Apricot Chutney*.

Makes 6 servings

Chut•ney *[chuht-nee]*

- noun

A sweet and sour condiment of East Indian origin. Comprised of fruit, herbs, spices and seasoning, chutney is often used as an accompaniment for hot and cold meats, fish and cheeses and is popular in western cuisine.

Apricot Chutney

2 (10 oz.) jars apricot jam

1 cup rice vinegar

¼ cup mustard seed

1 Tbsp. fresh ginger, minced (fresh ginger is preferred, but 1 tsp. dried ginger may be substituted)

Combine all ingredients in a medium skillet and bring to a boil over medium high heat. Reduce heat slightly and continue simmering, stirring frequently, until the mixture is thickened and reduced to 2 cups, about 8 – 10 minutes.

Allow to cool before serving. Store in an airtight container in the refrigerator.

Apricot Chutney will keep in the refrigerator as long as a jar of jam. Try topping toasted french baguette slices with cream cheese and a spoonful of chutney. It also pairs nicely with grilled chicken or fish. I like to grill a pork tenderloin and slice it thinly across the grain. I arrange the slices on a platter and drizzle the pork with the apricot chutney. Fabulous!

"Plant a radish, get a radish, never any doubt. That's why I love vegetables, you know what they're about."

– Tom Jones and Harvey Schmidt
Broadway writer and lyricist team

Salt Crusted New Potatoes

Harvested in the spring and summer, new potatoes are not a separate variety of potato, but simply a younger version of any kind of potato. The skin of new potatoes is thinner and flakier than that of older potatoes, and for that reason they are rarely peeled. This recipe calls for red skinned new potatoes, which have a white flesh that is waxy and flavorful. They are well suited for boiling and steaming.

Kosher salt is what I prefer for seasoning food after it has been cooked. It is much milder than regular table salt and has a flat, crystalline texture that allows it to adhere to most food, making your dish both flavorful and visually appetizing.

2 lbs. red skinned new potatoes
6 Tbsp. butter, melted
2 tsp. table salt
kosher salt

Gently scrub the new potatoes to remove any dirt. Place them in a large saucepan or pot and cover with water. Add the table salt and bring the water to a boil. Reduce the heat slightly and simmer 20–30 minutes or until the potatoes are fork tender. Drain the water from the pot. Pour the melted butter over the potatoes and toss gently so as not to break the skins. Transfer the potatoes to a serving bowl and sprinkle generously with kosher salt.

Makes 8 servings

Creamy Cole Slaw

Not being a cook who is fond of shredding cabbage, I am grateful for the abundance of shortcuts available to me when preparing a family dinner on a busy Sunday – or any day for that matter. Bagged coleslaw is one of my favorites. I use the tri-color variety, consisting of shredded green cabbage, purple cabbage and carrots. Jarred mayonnaise is fine, or opt for the homemade variety on p. 53.

2 bags tri-color cole slaw mix
1 ½ cup mayonnaise
½ cup sugar
3 Tbsp. white or cider vinegar
2 tsp. salt
1 medium onion, chopped
1 tsp. celery seed, optional

In a large bowl, combine mayonnaise, sugar, vinegar, salt and celery seed. Add the cole slaw mix and onions and toss to thoroughly coat with the dressing. Cover and refrigerate for at least an hour. Toss before serving.

Makes 8-10 servings

"*Never eat more than you can lift.*"

– Miss Piggy
  American puppet character

White Cheddar Cornbread

The introduction of pre seasoned cast iron skillets to the market means both new and experienced southern cooks don't have to spend months – or even years – conditioning and seasoning their skillets. They are ready to go right off the shelf. This delicious cornbread recipe, presented in a cast iron skillet, is certainly a southern Sunday classic.

1 ½ cups cornmeal

1 ½ cups all-purpose flour

1 cup sugar

2 eggs

1 ½ tsp. salt

5 tsp. baking powder

1 ½ cups milk

2/3 cup vegetable oil

1 cup yellow corn

1 cup white cheddar cheese, shredded

Preheat oven to 400 degrees. Generously spray a 10" cast iron skillet with cooking spray. *Note: a 9-inch round cake pan or square baking dish may be used. Cooking time will need to be increased slightly.*

In a large bowl, combine cornmeal, flour, sugar, salt and baking powder. Form a well in the center of the dry ingredients and add the eggs, milk and vegetable oil. Combine the wet ingredients and then gradually incorporate the dry ingredients. Add the corn and mix well.

Pour the batter into the greased skillet or baking pan. Bake for 20-25 minutes or until a toothpick inserted in the center comes out clean. Remove from the oven and sprinkle immediately with the cheese.

Makes 8-10 servings

Southern Key Lime Pie

Rich, creamy and full of zesty key lime flavor, this classic recipe is everyone's favorite. Key limes are smaller, more acidic, stronger tasting and slightly sweeter than standard limes. Their unique flavor is essential to this pie, therefore substituting regular lime juice is not recommended. Key lime juice is available next to the other lime juices in nearly every grocery store.

3 cups sweetened condensed milk

½ cup sour cream

¾ cup key lime juice

1 Tbsp. grated lime zest, plus more for garnishing

1 2/3 cups graham cracker crumbs

¼ cup sugar

6 Tbsp. butter, melted

1 pint whipping cream

¼ cup sugar

Preheat oven to 350 degrees.

In a bowl, combine graham cracker crumbs, sugar and butter. Press into the bottom and sides of a 9-inch pie plate. Pre-bake the crust for 8 minutes. Cool.

Combine condensed milk, sour cream, key lime juice and zest in a medium mixing bowl. Pour mixture into the graham cracker crust and bake for 8 more minutes.

Place the pie in the refrigerator and chill thoroughly, about 2-3 hours. Prior to serving, prepare the whipped cream topping. Place the whipping cream in the bowl of an electric stand mixer. Add the sugar and whip the cream until soft peaks form. Spread the cream over the top of the pie and garnish with grated key lime zest.

Makes 8 servings

"*Seize the moment. Remember all those women on the Titanic who waved off the dessert cart.*"

– Erma Bombeck (1927–1996)
American humorist and author

A Late Lunch and Yellow Lilies

The Menu

Sunday's Best Roast Chicken

Garden Fresh Skillet Tomatoes

Perfect Macaroni and Cheese

Sweet Vanilla Cupcakes with Butter Cream Frosting

"There is no sight on earth more appealing than the sight of a woman making dinner for someone she loves."

- Thomas Wolfe (1900-1938)
  American novelist

A Change of View

$\mathscr{I}$ have been known on occasion to set dinner tables in nontraditional places around my house. Fortunately, Sunday dinner need not be limited to the same location week after week. A new spot and a change of view can be a delightful change of pace and can enliven your Sunday dinner. A cozy corner of the den, a sunny spot on the front porch, and even a patch of grass under a backyard shade tree can all serve as unique dinner locations.

$\mathscr{O}$n this particular Sunday, I positioned a sturdy folding table in front of a fireplace and draped it to the floor with a yellow and white floral quilt. The focal point of the table is a fresh arrangement of yellow lilies and mini mums. Large white chef's plates, crisp white linen napkins and cut glassware create a light and elegant mood for our afternoon lunch.

"When you have only two pennies left in the world, buy a loaf of bread with one, and a lily with the other."

– Chinese Proverb

A Fresh Lily Centerpiece

This cheerful lily centerpiece is a snap to assemble and will cost a fraction of a pre-made arrangement. I purchase 6 to 8 cut Asian lilies, a batch of mini mums and sprays of tree fern for filler. Begin by selecting a vase. This white pedestal serving bowl works nicely with the yellow and white color scheme and provides height to give our arrangement a dramatic effect. Trim a block of florist foam to fit the size of the vase. Soak the foam according to the instructions and press it snugly into the vase (Fig. 1). Trim the lily stems diagonally, leaving longer stems for the top and shorter stems for the sides. Position the lilies evenly and press them firmly into the foam (Fig. 2). Repeat this procedure with the mini mums (Fig. 3). Insert the sprigs of tree fern throughout to fill any holes or gaps and to add height to your arrangement (Fig. 4).

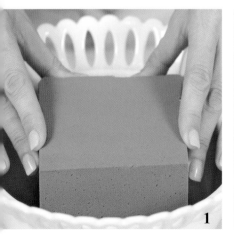

1

2

3

Five Spice Blend

This is a simple, full flavored spice blend for seasoning chicken or steak. I store mine in a shakeable glass jar where it's always close at hand.

½ cup kosher salt
¼ cup garlic powder
¼ cup onion powder
¼ cup paprika
3 Tbsp. black pepper

To wash, or not to wash?

Most chicken recipes no longer include instructions to wash the chicken before it is cooked. Research has shown there is a greater risk of cross contaminating something else in your kitchen in the process. Remember that any bacteria present will be killed when the chicken is cooked. Objects that come in contact with raw chicken should be washed immediately in hot, soapy water. I keep a separate cutting board in my kitchen that is strictly used for raw meat and poultry.

A Kitchen "Tough Guy"

Poultry shears are scissors that are specifically designed to cut through bone and other tough material. You'll feel a sense of power as this useful tool allows you to cut right through a whole chicken with ease. Lightweight and versatile, poultry shears are slightly bulkier than regular kitchen shears. I use mine in a variety of ways, including chopping herbs, trimming flower stems, and even cutting pizza.

How to Butterfly a Chicken

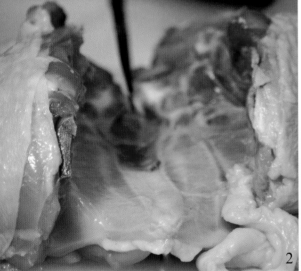

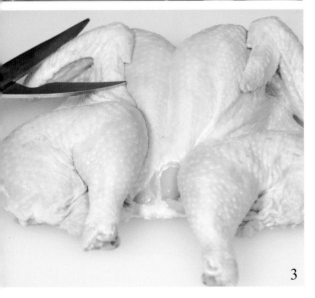

A relatively simple technique, butterflying involves removing the chicken's backbone so it may be opened up and laid flat during cooking. This process speeds the cooking time and results in a chicken that makes a lovely presentation and is easy to carve and serve. It is a helpful technique for both grilling and roasting poultry.

1. Place the chicken on a stable work surface with the legs facing away from you. Hold firmly to the tail, or flap of skin, at the end. Using poultry shears or a sharp knife, cut closely along the right side of the backbone (Fig. 1). Repeat procedure on the left side and remove the backbone.

2. Inside the cavity, locate the white piece of cartilage at the tip of the breastbone and cut through it (Fig. 2). Firmly grasp the sides of the chicken and bend it backward at the line of the cut. You may hear a crack.

3. Flip the chicken over and lay it flat (Fig. 3). Trim away any excess fat or skin.

" *If God grants me longer life, I will see to it that no peasant in my kingdom will lack the means to have a chicken in the pot every Sunday.*"

- Henri IV (1553–1610)
  King of France

Sunday's Best Roast Chicken

Roast chicken is traditionally a Sunday dinner favorite. This simple recipe is full of flavor and produces a succulent chicken with crispy skin.

1 (4–5 lb.) roasting chicken, butterflied *(see "How to Butterfly a Chicken, p. 131)*
olive oil for drizzling

Prepare a container of *Five Spice Blend (p. 130)*, or use the following:
4 tsp. kosher salt
2 tsp. garlic powder
2 tsp. onion powder
2 tsp. paprika
½ tsp. pepper

Preheat oven to 400 degrees.
Combine all the spices and set aside. Pat the chicken dry with paper towels and lay it, breast side up, in a roasting pan. *(Line the pan with aluminum foil for easy clean up).* Drizzle the chicken on both sides with olive oil. Sprinkle the chicken on both sides with the spice blend, rubbing it all over.

Roast the chicken until it is golden and crispy, about 45–55 minutes. A meat thermometer should read 165 degrees when inserted into the thickest part of the thigh. Loosely cover the chicken with aluminum foil and allow it to rest for 10 minutes.

A sharp knife will make short work of carving a butterflied chicken. Begin by slicing down the center to separate the two halves, discarding the breastbone. The leg and thigh will easily separate from the breast when sliced at an angle, although after roasting it may pull away with no effort at all. The chicken may then be served in quarters, or the breasts may be sliced and the legs may be separated from the thighs by cutting down firmly through the joint that connects them.

Makes 4–6 servings

Garden Fresh Skillet Tomatoes

I can thank my favorite aunt, and fabulous cook, Nita Jones of Auburndale, FL, for this wonderful tomato recipe. Just about any variety of firm tomato works well. I love taking advantage of the colorful heirloom tomatoes when they are in season. Served piping hot and infused with flavor from the marinade, these tomatoes pair beautifully with Sunday's Best Roast Chicken.

3–4 large, firm tomatoes, sliced thick
1 Tbsp. butter

Dressing:
2 Tbsp. olive oil
1 Tbsp. vinegar (red wine, balsamic or cider)
1 tsp. sugar
½ tsp. salt
2 cloves garlic, minced
2 Tbsp. parsley, chopped

Melt the butter in a large skillet over medium heat. Add the tomatoes in a single layer and cook for 5 minutes. While the tomatoes are cooking, whisk together the dressing ingredients in a small bowl. Turn the tomatoes once and pour the dressing over them. Simmer an additional 5 minutes.

Makes 4-6 servings

"It's difficult to think anything but pleasant thoughts while eating a homegrown tomato."

– Lewis Grizzard (1946–1994)
American writer and humorist

Three More Ways to Love a Tomato

If summer had a "flavor," it would likely be that of juicy, heirloom tomatoes. Those quintessential summer beauties are the "crown and glory" of the season – and the reason I often return from the farmer's market with far more tomatoes than my family could possibly eat in a week. Try showcasing their flavor with a simple tomato salad. Slice 3-4 tomatoes and arrange them on a platter. Coarsely chop one small tomato and place in a small bowl. Add 6 Tbsp. oil, 2 Tbsp. white wine vinegar, 1 tsp. sugar, 1/4 tsp. salt, and 1 Tbsp. chopped fresh Italian parsley. Toss the dressing until thoroughly combined, pressing on the chopped tomato with the back of a spoon to expel some of its juices. Spoon over the sliced tomatoes.
Makes 4-6 servings

I remember the first time I heard southern humorist, Ludlow Porch, on the radio, describing the proper way to eat a tomato sandwich. He said the tomato should preferably still be warm from the garden. Only white bread must be used, as well as real mayonnaise and a sprinkling of salt. He described the importance of leaning over the kitchen sink while eating it because the juices will inevitable run down your cheeks. According to Ludlow, eating a tomato sandwich this way is an experience that is blissfully southern. I whole heartedly agree.

Deliciously simple, tomato and mozzarella salads might come under the heading of favorite *new* southern cuisine, for nearly every southern woman I know adores them. Try a simple technique for chopping basil by first rolling the leaves (Fig. 1) and then slicing them crosswise (Fig. 2). Alternate thick slices of ripe red tomato and fresh mozzarella, then top with the basil. Drizzle with olive oil and balsamic vinegar. Sprinkle with kosher salt and pepper and enjoy. A loaf of crusty French bread makes a nice accompaniment

"Food, like a loving touch or a glimpse of divine power, has that ability to comfort."

- Norman Kolpas
  American author

Perfect Macaroni and Cheese

The addition of Gruyere cheese to this macaroni and cheese recipe (which actually calls for penne pasta, not macaroni) gives it a delectably complex cheese flavor.

1 lb. dry penne pasta

4 cups milk

½ lb. (1 stick) butter

1 Tbsp. dry mustard

½ cup all purpose flour

12 oz. sharp cheddar cheese, grated

12 oz. Gruyere cheese, grated

1 medium onion, finely chopped

Topping:

1 ½ cup panko breadcrumbs

4 Tbsp. butter, melted

Preheat oven to 375 degrees.

In a pot of boiling, salted water, cook the penne pasta according to directions.

In a large pot, melt the butter. Add the flour and cook, stirring with a whisk, for 2 minutes. Whisk in the milk, onion and dry mustard and continue cooking over medium high heat until the mixture is thick and smooth. Remove from the heat and add the cheese, stirring with a spoon until the cheese melts. Add the drained pasta to the cheese mixture and toss gently. Pour into a greased 3–4 quart baking dish.

Combine the breadcrumbs and melted butter and sprinkle on top. Bake for 30 minutes.

Makes 12 servings

*W*ho doesn't love cupcakes? Those little culinary confections are also known as "fairy cakes," a fanciful reference to their diminutive size. Cupcakes evolved in the United States during the 19th century. Prior to the development of muffin tins, cupcakes were baked in individual pottery cups, hence the name *cupcake*. Cooks appreciated the simplicity of the preparation and the quick baking time compared to traditional cakes. The appeal of cupcakes has not waned over the years. In fact, they have experienced a recent surge in popularity as many adults have rediscovered a fondness for this charming childhood treat.

Sweet Vanilla Cupcakes with Butter Cream Frosting

2 ½ cups all purpose flour

1 ½ tsp. baking powder

½ tsp. baking soda

1 tsp. salt

1 cup vegetable or canola oil

2 cups sugar

3 eggs

2 tsp. pure vanilla extract

1 cup sour cream

Preheat oven to 350 degrees.

Line two 12-cup cupcake pans with cupcake papers. In a small bowl, sift together the flour, baking powder, baking soda and salt. Set aside. In the bowl of a stand mixer, beat the sugar and eggs until light and creamy. Add the oil, vanilla and sour cream and mix well. Gradually, add the flour mixture. Continue mixing on medium speed until smooth. Pour the batter into the prepared cupcake pans and bake 18–20 minutes or until a toothpick inserted in the center comes out clean. Cool completely before icing.

Butter Cream Frosting

3 cups confectioner's sugar

1 cup (2 sticks) butter, room temperature

1 ½ tsp. pure vanilla extract

2 Tbsp. whipping cream

In the bowl of a stand mixer with a whisk attachment, cream the sugar and butter on low speed. Increase to medium speed and mix for 2-3 minutes. Add the vanilla and 1 Tbsp. of the cream. Continue mixing, adding more cream if necessary to achieve the proper spreading consistency.

A Cozy Family Gathering

The Menu

Citrus Glazed Baked Ham

Chunky Brown Sugar Sweet Potatoes

Simple Sauteed Green Beans with Sesame Seeds

Sour Cream Pound Cake with Pineapple Compote

"All great change in America begins at the dinner table."

– Ronald Reagan (1911–2004)
40th President of the United States

The Aroma of Home

Our sense of smell is powerful in its abilty to enhance our mood and bring distant memories - particularly those from our childhood - to the forefront of our minds once again. The sweet scent of gardenias on a breeze or the aroma of a hearty beef roast simmering in the oven may instantly transport us back to a familiar place and time when we were young and all seemed right with the world.

$\mathcal{T}$hose with large families like mine may not find many chances for smaller, more intimate, dinner settings. Yet when the opportunity arises, I love taking advantage of it by creating a cozier version of Sunday dinner for just two or three. On this particular, chilly Sunday afternoon, I cleared the family photos from a round, antique oak table and shifted it toward the windows to capture the waning hours of winter sunlight. I pulled an assortment of old black Windsor chairs to the table and then filled an antique crock with a small winter fern for a touch of fresh greenery. The sweet, hickory smell of Citrus Glazed Baked Ham filled the air. Chunky sweet potatoes, sauteed green beans and sour cream pound cake completed a simple, yet deliciously hearty menu for our Cozy Family Gathering.

All About Ham

For a pork product to be called *ham*, it must come from the hind leg of a hog. Meat from the hog's front leg is referred to as *pork shoulder picnic*. Ham may be purchased fresh or cured. Fresh ham must be cooked prior to eating, while cured ham does not require heating and may be eaten right from the package. Dry curing involves rubbing fresh ham with salt and other ingredients and allowing it to age for several weeks to a year. It produces a salty product and is the method used for country ham and prosciutto. Wet curing, or brine curing, is the most popular method of producing ham. The ham is injected with a solution of salt, sugar, nitrates, nitrites and other flavorings. After the curing process, a ham may be either cooked or smoked. Smoking is a process that involves hanging the ham in a smokehouse where it absorbs the flavor of the smoke from smoldering flames. This prolongs the shelf life of the ham, adds flavor and produces a deeper, redder color.

"There is no place more delightful than one's own fireplace."

- Marcus Tullius Cicero (106 BC – 43 BC)
  Roman philosopher, statesman and orator

A pig and a chicken were on their way to dinner.
The pig asked, "What would you like to eat?"
The chicken replied, "I'd like ham and eggs."
The pig contemplated his friend's answer for a moment, then replied,
"Well, that's just fine for you. It's a small donation on your part,
but it's a total sacrifice for me!"

Citrus Glazed Baked Ham

Few things rival the sweet and smoky aroma of a succulent baked ham. It will always be a featured attraction on any Sunday dinner table. I typically purchase a bigger ham than I need, just so I can be sure to have plenty of delicious leftovers for ham sandwiches. Although safe to eat at any temperature, a precooked ham will taste best when heated to an internal temperature of 140 degrees.

1 (6–8 lb.) fully cooked, bone–in ham
1 (18 oz.) jar orange marmalade
1 cup orange juice
½ cup spicy brown mustard
½ tsp. ground ginger
¼ tsp. ground cloves
¼ tsp. ground nutmeg

Preheat oven to 350 degrees.
Place ham, fat side up, in a large baking pan lined with aluminum foil.

In a small bowl, combine the marmalade, orange juice, mustard, ginger, cloves and nutmeg. Pour 1 cup of the orange sauce over the ham. Set aside the remaining sauce. Place the ham on the lowest oven rack and bake for 12–13 minutes per pound, or about 1 ½ hours for a 7 lb. ham. Baste the ham with the drippings once or twice during cooking. Allow the ham to rest for 15 minutes before carving. While the ham is resting, transfer the orange sauce to a small saucepan and warm over medium low heat. Serve the orange sauce alongside the ham.

Makes 12–14 servings

Chunky Brown Sugar Sweet Potatoes

Rather than boiling and mashing the sweet potatoes, as is traditionally done, this recipe calls for cutting the potatoes into chunks, tossing them with butter and brown sugar, and roasting them . The result is a deep, sticky-sweet, caramelized sweet potato flavor, and a perfect compliment to Citrus Glazed Baked Ham.

4–6 large sweet potatoes

6 Tbsp. butter, melted

½ cup brown sugar, packed

Preheat oven to 350 degrees.

Peel the sweet potatoes and cut them into ½-inch chunks. Place them in a large, shallow baking pan.

In a small saucepan, melt the butter over medium heat. Add the brown sugar and stir until the sugar is dissolved. Pour the mixture over the sweet potatoes and toss to coat thoroughly. Bake for 1 – 1 ½ hours, tossing once or twice. Potatoes will beome slightly sticky and may brown around the edges slightly as they caramelize.

Makes 6–8 servings

Simple Sauteed Green Beans with Sesame Seeds

I select my sesame seeds from the Asian foods aisle of my grocery store, where they are typically much cheaper than the spice aisle.

1 ½ lbs. fresh green beans, stem ends removed

1 tsp. salt

2 Tbsp. olive oil

1 Tbsp. sesame seeds

Place green beans and salt in a large skillet, cover with water and bring to a boil. Cook for 4–5 minutes, until crisp tender. Drain the green beans and return them to the skillet. Add sesame seeds and olive oil, tossing to coat. Saute over medium high heat for 3–4 minutes or until green beans are fully cooked and sesame seeds are golden.

Makes 8 servings

Old Fashioned Sour Cream Pound Cake with Pineapple Compote

After years of trying pound cake recipes, I have finally decided to settle on this one. It will likely be the only recipe for pound cake I will ever use. It has been adapted from an old family recipe. I doubled the amount of sour cream called for in the original recipe to make the sour cream flavor more discernable. The nice thing about pound cake is that it will soak up the flavor and juices of whatever fruit you choose to top it with. The pineapple compote in this recipe is a deliciously sweet addition.

3 cups all purpose flour

1 tsp. baking soda

1 tsp. salt

3 cups sugar

6 eggs

1 cup (2 sticks) butter

1 Tbsp. pure vanilla extract

1 (16 oz.) container sour cream

Preheat oven to 325 degrees. Grease and flour a tube pan. In a small bowl, sift together flour, baking soda and salt. In a large bowl, combine the butter and sugar until creamy. Add the vanilla, sour cream, and eggs, one at a time, beating after each addition. Add the flour, one cup at a time, until fully incorporated. Pour into the prepared tube pan and bake for 1 hour, or until a toothpick inserted in the center comes out clean. Cool for 30 minutes and then invert the cake onto a serving plate. Top individual slices with the pineapple compote.   *Makes 12 servings*

Pineapple Compote:

4 cups fresh pineapple, diced

½ cup golden raisins

2 Tbsp. Butter

¼ cup brown sugar, firmly packed

¾ cup pineapple juice

Combine all ingredients in a medium saucepan and cook over medium heat, stirring occasionally, until reduced by half. Spoon compote over individual slices of pound cake. Also delicious served over vanilla ice cream.

A Hearty Outdoor Dinner

The Menu

Southern Home Style Meatloaf with Sweet Chili Glaze

Three Cheese Smashed Potatoes

Lemon-Sweet Cucumbers with Onion and Dill

Brown Sugar Brownies

"We should look for someone to eat and drink with before looking for something to eat and drink."

– Epicurus (341–270 BC)
  Greek philosopher

Dinner on the Deck

$\mathscr{D}$ ining outdoors is a particularly enjoyable experience when the weather is beautiful and the air is fresh. The transitional weeks of autumn, when the temperatures are beginning to cool, provide wonderful opportunities for al fresco dinners. A black mesh wrought iron dining table and chairs *(opposite, top left),* more than 60 years old and doing fine, is my location of choice. The focal point of the table is the old brown crock filled with Shasta daisies and sprays of golden solidago *(opposite, bottom).* Warm, savory dishes like Southern Home Style Meatloaf and Three Cheese Smashed Potatoes pair nicely with Lemon-Sweet Cucumbers to satisfy those hearty autumn appetites.

Kettles and Buckets and Crocks, Oh My...

*T*hink outside the vase when it comes to displaying your beautiful seasonal blooms. My theory is that if it has a hole or an opening, you can stick flowers in it. Try selecting a variety of blooms within a common color scheme and displaying them in a group, using an assortment of creative - even whimsical - containers. Here, I've filled an old wooden water pail with bronze chrysanthemums and given a bouquet of Shasta daisies a new home in a favorite copper tea kettle. The old brown jug holds orange spray roses and sprigs of eucalyptus. Tinted carnations and hypericum berries fill a little brown and white crock, while an antique spool provides the perfect spot to showcase a pair of deep orange Gerbera daisies.

"Food is the most primitive form of comfort."

- Sheilah Graham (1904–1988)

Columnist during Hollywood's "Golden Age"

Southern Home Style Meatloaf with Sweet Chili Glaze

You can enjoy this hearty meatloaf twice as much if you have enough left over for meatloaf sandwiches the next day. I prepare the sandwiches on white bread with a little mayonnaise, a sprinkle of kosher salt and leafy green lettuce. Delicious.

2 lbs. ground chuck

1 lb. mild pork sausage

½ medium onion, finely chopped

½ medium green pepper, finely chopped

2 Tbsp. Worcestershire sauce

2 tsp. salt

½ tsp. pepper

3 cloves garlic, minced

1 egg

1 ½ cups milk

1 ½ cups breadcrumbs

1 bottle chili sauce

¼ cup brown sugar, packed

1 Tbsp. Italian parsley, chopped

Preheat oven to 350 degrees.

In a large bowl, combine the ground chuck and Italian sausage. Add the onion, green pepper, Worcestershire sauce, salt, pepper and garlic. In a separate small bowl, beat the egg and milk together and then add them to the meat mixture. Add the bread crumbs. Using your hands, mix the meatloaf mixture until it is thoroughly combined. Place it into a shallow baking pan and shape it into a loaf. In a small bowl, combine the chili sauce and brown sugar. Pour ½ cup of the chili sauce over the meatloaf and reserve the rest. Bake the meatloaf for 60–70 minutes. Let rest 10–15 minutes before carving. Sprinkle the parsley over the top and serve with the remaining chili glaze.

Makes 8–10 servings

Three Cheese Smashed Potatoes

This deliciously cheesy potato dish uses unpeeled potatoes that are "smashed" to create a chunky, hearty texture. Be sure to use baby or new potatoes, which have skins that are tender and thin.

1 ½ – 2 lbs. baby Yukon gold or red new potatoes
¼ cup (1/2 stick) butter
½ tsp. salt
1/3 cup chicken broth
½ cup sharp cheddar cheese, shredded
½ cup Monterrey Jack cheese, shredded
4 oz. cream cheese
3 – 4 green onions, sliced

Place potatoes in a medium pot and cover with cold water. Bring to a boil and cook over medium high heat for 12–15 minutes or until potatoes are fork tender. Drain. Using a potato masher or the back of a wooden spoon, "smash" the potatoes into large chunks.

Place cream cheese and butter in a microwave safe bowl and soften at 50% power for 60–90 seconds. Combine with the chicken broth and salt and whisk until smooth. Pour the mixture over the hot potatoes and toss. Add the cheddar and Monterrey Jack cheese and toss gently. Transfer the potatoes to a serving bowl and sprinkle with the green onions.

Makes 8 servings

Lemon-Sweet Cucumbers with Onion and Dill

Infused with a sweet, lemon vinaigrette, this refreshing salad is a light and flavorful accompaniment to heavier dishes.

½ cup sugar

½ tsp. salt

½ tsp. dried dill

½ tsp. lemon peel, grated

½ cup vinegar

1 Tbsp. lemon juice

2 large cucumbers, sliced into ¼–inch pieces, then sliced in half

½ red onion, thinly sliced

In a medium bowl, whisk together the first six ingredients.
Add the cucumber slices to the bowl and toss. Cover and refrigerate 4
hours to overnight.

Makes 6 servings

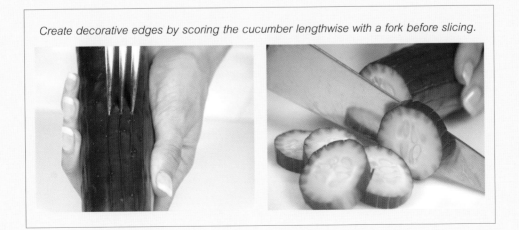

Create decorative edges by scoring the cucumber lengthwise with a fork before slicing.

Brown Sugar Brownies

Light or dark brown sugar may be used in these delectably chewy, old fashioned brownies.

2 Tbsp. butter

2 eggs

1 cup brown sugar, packed

5 Tbsp. flour

¼ tsp. baking soda

1 cup pecans, chopped

1 tsp. pure vanilla extract

Preheat oven to 350 degrees.

Melt butter in a 9–inch square baking pan by placing it in the oven or microwave. In a small bowl, beat the eggs and vanilla. In a separate bowl, combine the brown sugar, flour, baking soda and pecans. Add the egg mixture and stir well. Pour the batter on top of the butter in the baking pan. Do not stir. Bake for 20 minutes. Let cool for 10–15 minutes and then flip, upside down, onto a cooling rack. Dust with powdered sugar.

Makes 12 servings

"You don't have to cook fancy or complicated masterpieces - just good food from fresh ingredients."

- Julia Child (1912-2004)
  American chef, author and television personality

Ten Southern Classics

Buttermilk Biscuits

Deviled Eggs

Fried Blackberry Pies

Nine Hour Barbecue Ribs

Sweet Iced Tea

Home Style Lemonade

Collard Greens with Hickory Smoked Bacon

Strawberry Freezer Jam

Classic Potato Salad

Peach Bread Pudding

Buttermilk Biscuits

Biscuit making is not a difficult task, but is certainly serious business for many southern cooks. After all, homemade biscuits are perhaps the most quintessentially southern comfort food. The process by which the biscuits are prepared is equally as important as the ingredients used. Once you understand the technique, a little practice is all that is required to become a master biscuit maker. One of the age old questions regarding biscuits is whether to use butter or shortening. In general, shortening produces biscuits that are tender and dense, while butter yields a biscuit that is flaky and very flavorful. Either one will produce a classic, southern style biscuit, though I have opted for the butter recipe. Here are some important biscuit tips:

1. Keep the buttermilk and butter cold. The goal is to develop biscuit dough that has small bits of butter coated in flour. This is key to creating a light, flaky biscuit. If the butter is too warm, it will blend with the flour and become too smooth to rise properly. Work quickly so the heat from your hands does not warm the dough.

2. Gluten is the enemy of a perfect biscuit, therefore overworking the biscuit dough should be avoided at all costs. Gluten is developed as the dough is handled or kneaded and results in a biscuit that is overly dense and tough. By patting the dough, and not kneading it, the flat layers of butter remain intact and will rise to create a light, flaky texture.

3. When cutting out the biscuits, be sure to press straight down with the biscuit cutter and do not twist. This will help keep those butter layers intact.

4. By baking at a high temperature, the biscuit dough will set quickly and yield a biscuit that is nicely browned on top and bottom with white sides.

4 cups all purpose flour
½ tsp. baking soda
2 Tbsp. baking powder
2 tsp. salt
1 Tbsp. sugar
¾ cup (1 ½ sticks) cold butter
1 ½ cups buttermilk

Preheat oven to 450 degrees. In a large mixing bowl, combine the flour, baking soda, baking powder, salt and sugar. Cut the cold butter into small chunks and, using a pastry cutter, two knives, or a food processor, cut the butter into the flour mixture until it resembles course meal. Add the buttermilk and mix just until combined. Do not overwork. Turn the dough out onto a well floured surface. Gently pat the dough to a thickness of ½-inch. Do not knead or use a rolling pin. Cut out the biscuits using a round cutter (don't twist) and place them on a baking sheet. For slightly crispy edges, place the biscuits 1 inch apart. For softer edges, place them so their edges are touching one another. Bake 9–10 minutes depending on size, or until the biscuits are golden. Serve warm with butter and jam.

Makes 12–16 servings

Deviled Eggs

Deviled eggs are a popular southern favorite at any picnic, potluck or family get together. They are so loved at my house, I typically have to hide them in the back of the refrigerator or they will be gone before dinnertime.

12 hard boiled eggs
2 Tbsp. sweet pickle relish
4 Tbsp. mayonnaise
1 Tbsp. yellow mustard
¼ tsp. salt
paprika for garnish

Slice the hard boiled eggs in half lengthwise. Remove the yolks, place them in a small bowl and set the whites aside. With the back of a fork, mash the yolks to a crumbly texture. Add the pickle relish, mayonnaise, mustard and salt. Mix until well combined. Spoon the yolk mixture into the egg whites and sprinkle with paprika. Arrange the eggs on a serving platter.

Makes 24 servings

Fried Blackberry Pies

4 cups fresh or frozen blackberries

½ cup water

1 cup sugar

2 ½ Tbsp. cornstarch

4 cups all purpose flour

2 tsp. salt

1 Tbsp. sugar

1 cup milk

1 cup shortening

canola oil for frying

1 cup confectioner's sugar

4 Tbsp. water

In a saucepan over medium high heat, whisk together the water, 1 cup sugar and cornstarch. Add the berries and bring the mixture to a boil. Reduce heat slightly and continue cooking, stirring occasionally, until thickened, about 10 minutes. Set aside and allow to cool completely. Mixture will continue to thicken as it cools.

In a mixing bowl, combine the flour, salt, and 1 Tbsp. sugar. Cut in the shortening until the mixture resembles coarse meal. Add the milk and mix until the dough forms a ball. Turn the dough out onto a floured surface and roll to a thickness of about 1/4-inch. Cut the dough into 6-inch circles. I use a small bowl that is 6-inches in diameter to cut the circles. Depending on the size of your work surface, you may need to divide the dough in half and work it in two separate batches. Use extra flour as needed to prevent the dough from sticking.

Place a spoonful of blackberry filling in the center of each dough circle. Fold the circle in half and use a fork to press and seal the edges.

Heat the vegetable oil in a large skillet over medium heat until hot, but not smoking. Fry the pies in a single layer, leaving space between them, for 1-2 minutes per side or until golden brown. Drain the pies on paper towels.

In a small bowl, combine the powdered sugar and water to form a thin glaze. Brush the tops of the pies with the glaze.

Makes 16-18 servings

Ultimate 9 Hour Barbecue Ribs

I think these are the best tasting ribs on earth. The recipe is based on one I enjoyed tremendously one 4th of July at the home of my brother and sister-in-law, Phil and Laura Wahlbom. Few things are worth a nine hour wait, but these ribs are definitely one of them. Pop them in the oven in the morning and they will be ready by dinnertime. The sweet, tangy, smokey flavor of these fall-off-the-bone ribs makes them the ultimate "feel good" food. The secret is in the sauce – and the extra long cooking time.

2 full racks baby back ribs	½ cup honey
2 cloves garlic, minced	½ cup apple cider vinegar
1 medium onion, finely chopped	½ cup pineapple juice
6 Tbsp. butter	2 Tbsp. Worcestershire sauce
2 ½ cups ketchup or chili sauce	1 Tbsp. chili powder
1 cup brown sugar, packed	3 tsp. salt
3 Tbsp. spicy mustard w/ horseradish	1 ½ tsp. cayenne pepper
½ cup dark corn syrup	1 t. black pepper

Preheat oven to 190 degrees.

In a medium saucepan, melt butter and cook garlic and onion until soft. Add all remaining sauce ingredients, bring to a boil, reduce heat and simmer 30 minutes, stirring occasionally. Let cool.

Cut baby back rib racks in half, layer them in a large baking pan and cover with a generous amount of sauce. Cover tightly with aluminum foil and bake for 9 hours. Discard the drippings and serve the ribs with the extra barbecue sauce.

Makes 6-8 servings

Sweet Iced Tea

Southerners have had a long standing love affair with sweet tea. Typically, it is served over ice and consumed any time of day. In fact, no southerner would ever balk at the idea of having a chicken biscuit and sweet iced tea for breakfast. Usually found in gallon pitchers on the top shelf of most southern refrigerators, sweet tea can easily carry the hefty title of "elixir of the south."

4 quart–size tea bags
2 cups sugar

In a large saucepan, bring 3 quarts of water to a boil. Add the sugar and stir until it dissolves. Add the tea bags, cover, and steep for 20 minutes. Pour the tea into a gallon pitcher and fill the rest with cold water or ice. Chill in the refrigerator. Serve over ice and garnish with lemon slices and mint, if desired.

Makes 1 gallon

"Iced tea is too pure and natural a creation not to have been invented as soon as tea, ice, and hot weather crossed paths."

- John Egerton
  American author

Home Style Lemonade

Cool, tart and refreshing, lemonade is another favorite "any time of year" southern beverage. Roll the lemons on the counter with your hands before squeezing to help release the juices. A hand held lemon juicer will make the task much easier.

2 cups fresh lemon juice, equivalent to the juice of about 14 large lemons
1 2/3 cups sugar
8 cups cold water
lemon slices for garnish

In a small saucepan, heat 1 cup of the water and the sugar. Bring to a boil and stir to dissolve the sugar. Remove the syrup from the heat and cool.

In a pitcher, combine the lemon juice, the syrup and the remaining 7 cups of cold water. Refrigerate until chilled. Garnish with lemon slices and serve.

Makes 8–10 servings

Collard Greens with Hickory Smoked Bacon

2 lbs. collard greens, washed, thick stems removed, cut into bite size pieces

6 strips thick–sliced, hickory smoked bacon, cut into small pieces

1 medium onion, chopped

2 cloves garlic, minced

3 Tbsp. sugar

2 tsp. salt

¼ cup cider vinegar

1 ½ cups chicken broth

In a large stockpot over medium heat, fry bacon until golden but still soft. Add the onion and cook until soft and translucent. Add the garlic and saute until golden, about 1 minute. Add the sugar, salt and cider vinegar. Simmer until the liquid is reduced by about half. Add the collard greens and chicken broth. Cover and simmer until the greens are tender, about 60 minutes. Serve with the pan juices and a dash of hot sauce, if desired.

Makes 8 servings

Strawberry Freezer Jam

1 quart fresh strawberries, washed and stems removed

4 cups sugar

¾ cup water

1 box fruit pectin

Thoroughly wash, rinse and dry enough mason jars or plastic freezer containers to hold 5 cups of jam. Coarsely chop and then crush the strawberries. Measure exactly 2 cups of crushed strawberries into a bowl. Add the sugar and toss.

In a saucepan over high heat, bring the water and the pectin to a boil. Cook, stirring constantly, for 2 minutes. Add to the strawberries and continue stirring until the sugar is dissolved. Carefully pour the jam into the prepared jars or freezer containers and fill to ½-inch from the top. Wipe the tops of the jars and replace the lids. Let the jam sit at room temperature for 24 hours. Use jam within 3 weeks or store in the freezer for up to 1 year.

Makes 5 cups

"*This special feeling towards fruit, its glory and abundance, is I would say universal. We respond to strawberry fields or cherry orchards with a delight that a cabbage patch or even an elegant vegetable garden cannot provoke.*"

- Jane Grigson (1928–1990)
British cookery author

Classic Potato Salad

2 lbs. medium potatoes (about 5-6 potatoes), peeled and cut into large chunks

3/4 cup mayonnaise

½ cup sour cream

1 Tbsp. vinegar

1 ½ tsp. salt

½ t. garlic powder

2 tsp. dry mustard

Bring a large pot of salted water to a boil. Add the potatoes and cook until tender, but still firm, about 12-14 minutes.

In a mixing bowl, combine mayonnaise, sour cream, vinegar, salt, garlic powder and dry mustard. Drain the potatoes and while still hot, add them to the bowl. Toss gently. Serve warm or refrigerate for 1-2 hours and serve chilled. Garnish with sliced tomatoes and chopped chives, if desired.

Makes 6-8 servings

Peach Bread Pudding

This delectably sweet bread pudding recipe calls for challah bread rather than traditional white bread. The higher egg content in the challah results in a richer, more flavorful pudding.

1 large loaf challah bread, cut into cubes

2 cups heavy cream

2 cups milk

5 eggs

1 ½ cups sugar

1 tsp. cinnamon

1 (29 oz) can peaches in heavy syrup, drained and pureed until smooth in blender or food processor.

Preheat oven to 350 degrees.

In large bowl, whisk together cream, milk, eggs, sugar, cinnamon and pureed peaches. Add bread cubes and toss gently to coat. Let sit for 15 minutes.

Lightly coat a 10 x 14-inch baking pan with butter or cooking spray. Pour bread and egg mixture into pan and press gently. Bake 50–60 minutes or until a toothpick inserted in the center comes out clean. Serve warm or room temperature with Peach Syrup.

Makes 12 servings

Peach Syrup

1 ½ pounds fresh peaches, peeled and pitted – or 1 (29 oz.) can sliced peaches in heavy syrup

½ cup sugar

1 Tbsp. butter, melted

In a blender or food processor, puree peaches, sugar and butter until smooth. Syrup can be served warm or room temperature.

Recipe Index

Kitchen Techniques and Table Tips

Special Thanks

MY WONDERFUL FAMILY

*

NOAH MAIER, PHOTOGRAPHER

*

JUDY WAHLBOM

*

PAMELA SANDERS

*

FRED AND NITA JONES

*

THE WAHLBOM FAMILY

*

CHRIS AND KIM MAIOCCO, HIS KIDS PUBLISHING, INC.